GO FACTS NATURAL DISASTERS
Earthquake

A & C BLACK • LONDON

Earthquake

contents

© Blake Publishing 2006
Additional material © A & C Black Publishers Ltd 2006

First published in Australia in 2006 by Blake Education Pty Ltd

This edition published in the United Kingdom in 2006 by
A & C Black Publishers Ltd, 38 Soho Square, London W1D 3HB
www.acblack.com

Published by permission of Blake Publishing Pty Ltd, Leichhardt NSW, Australia.

Hardback edition
ISBN-10: 0-7136-7957-3
ISBN-13: 978-0-7136-7957-1

Paperback edition
ISBN-10: 0-7136-7965-4
ISBN-13: 978-0-7136-7965-6

A CIP record for this book is available from the British Library.

Written by Ian Rohr
Publisher: Katy Pike
Editor: Paul O'Beirne
Design and layout by The Modern Art Production Group

Photo credits: p5 (bl, br), p7 tr, bl, br), p9 (tr, br), p11 (top, bl, br), p13 (tl, tr,
bl), p15 (bl, br), p17 (top, bl, br), p19 (top, bl, br), p21 (tl, bl, br), p25 (bl, br)
(australian picture library); pp26–27 (Paul McEvoy).

Printed in China by WKT Company Ltd.

WARNING!

TSUNAMI HAZARD ZONE

AVIATION

What is an Earthquake?

Most earthquakes occur along fault lines in the Earth's crust. When sections of rock slip or move suddenly, this causes shock waves to travel long distances. These vibrating shock waves are what we know as an earthquake.

Fault lines

The constant movement of **tectonic plates** has its greatest impact along **fault lines**. Fault lines occur where these massive plates move against each other or where they pull apart. When sections of rock slip suddenly, an earthquake occurs, causing surface movements ranging from tremors, shaking ground, falling buildings to huge ocean waves.

The place underground where the rock moved is called the **focus**, or hypocentre, of the earthquake. The spot directly above the focus on the surface is known as the **epicentre** of the quake. The vibrations travel away from the focus of the quake in all directions through ground rock and ocean water.

How many?

Scientists estimate that over 1 500 000 earthquakes occur on Earth each year. Of these, over 100 000 can be felt. Only about 150 quakes per year cause any damage. Surface movements are **monitored** by instruments such as the **seismograph**, which measures the **magnitude** of each quake.

Major earthquakes reduce cities to rubble and cause landslides, floods, fires and giant **tsunami** waves. Quakes kill thousands of people every year and have caused an **estimated** 13 million deaths in the last 4000 years.

The word 'tectonic' comes from the Greek word 'tektonikos' which means buildings and other structures. Scientists use the word 'tectonics' to refer to the structures that make up the Earth's surface.

Earthquakes can vary from a mild tremor to the violent shaking and buckling of the Earth's surface.

The 1964 Anchorage, Alaska earthquake dropped buildings and roads 9 metres in some places, while in others it raised them 10 metres. It measured 9.2 on the Richter scale.

GO FACT!

DID YOU KNOW?

The Earth's surface is made up of large plates, called tectonic plates. These plates fit together like a giant jigsaw puzzle. They are unstable and are constantly moving. This movement causes most of the world's earthquakes and volcanoes, and changes the face of our planet.

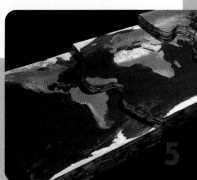

What Causes Earthquakes?

Most earthquakes are caused by the movement of tectonic plates. This movement can create enormous pressure. Earthquakes occur when this pressure is released.

Under pressure

As tectonic plates move, rock is pulled apart and pushed together. This creates **stress** in the rock. Rock is **brittle** and with enough force, will eventually break, slip or shift. When this occurs, all the stored energy is released. This release of energy causes the surrounding rock to vibrate.

These vibrations travel through and around the Earth, just like the ripples on a pond when a pebble drops into water. Much of this cracking and moving occurs slowly, but if the rock shifts or breaks suddenly, a major earthquake can result. The sudden release of **immense** pressure releases huge amounts of energy. The magnitude of the quake is a measure of how much energy was released.

Fault lines

Fault lines are cracks, or fractures, created by shifting rock layers and the movement of plates. They can range from small faults, such as cracks in cliff faces, to huge valleys running for thousands of kilometres. It is the movement of plates along large fault lines that leads to most of the world's earthquakes.

The movement of **magma** underneath volcanoes can also trigger earthquakes. At least 1–2 earthquakes are recorded at Mount Fuji every month.

A plate movement of 20 cm can be enough to set off a major earthquake, such as the 1995 Kobe earthquake in Japan which measured 6.9 on the Richter scale.

California's San Andreas fault is over 1000 km (621 miles) long and runs close to the major cities of Los Angeles and San Francisco.

GO FACT!

DID YOU KNOW?
Africa's Great Rift Valley is a huge fault line that runs for over 4000 km (2485 miles).

What Happens During an Earthquake?

During a severe earthquake, the ground moves and buckles, pipes burst, buildings collapse and roads twist and crack. All of these events are caused by shock waves spreading through and across the Earth.

Shock waves

The vibrations caused by an earthquake travel out from the focus – the point where the rock breaks or slips – in a series of shock waves. There are three main types of shock waves – primary, secondary and surface waves.

Primary (P) waves

These are the fastest travelling shock waves – 8 km per second (5 miles per second). They push and pull at the rock in the ground, but tend to cause little damage. They also create vibrations in the air that lead to the loud roaring noise often reported just before the shaking motion of an earthquake begins.

Secondary (S) waves

S-waves move more slowly than P-waves – 4.5 km per second (2.8 miles per second) – but result in more damage. They cause **subterranean** rock layers to move up and down or from side to side in a ripple-like motion.

Surface waves

These only occur on the Earth's surface and travel at about 1.5 km per second (0.9 miles per second). These waves cause the Earth's surface to buckle and heave. Surface waves can cause major damage far away from the epicentre – the point on the Earth's surface that lies directly above the earthquake's focus.

Earthquakes can cause the surface of the Earth to crack open. These surface fissures are rarely big enough to swallow people as shown in disaster movies.

People witnessed ground waves up to a metre high moving across the land like giant ripples during the 1906 Californian earthquake.

Shock waves are also known as seismic waves – this term comes from the Greek word 'seismos', meaning 'trembling earth'.

GO FACT!

DID YOU KNOW?

Shock waves from a 1923 earthquake started over 200 fires which destroyed 65% of the Japanese city of Tokyo, 80 kilometres (50 miles) away from the quake's epicentre.

Aftershocks

The violent shaking of an earthquake is over in less than a minute. But danger still lurks in the form of destructive aftershocks.

Aftershocks are smaller quakes occurring after an earthquake in the same area. Major earthquakes always have aftershocks. As the rocks at, or near, the earthquake's focus continue to move, they cause aftershocks. Some of these are as dangerous as the original earthquake.

Delayed danger

Aftershocks vary enormously in their **intensity**. Some may not be felt at all whereas others are major events. Some aftershocks do more damage than the quake that started them off. Following a large earthquake, aftershocks can continue at a low level for years.

After an earthquake it is important for survivors to get to open ground. Aftershocks can cause already damaged buildings to completely collapse. These also hamper rescue efforts as the already difficult work of finding survivors is made more dangerous.

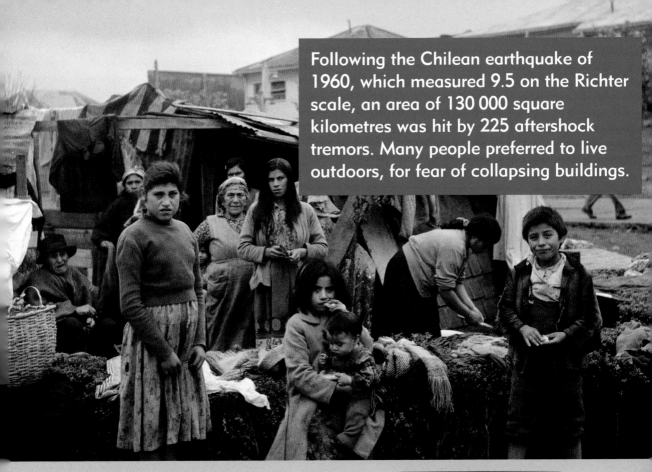

Following the Chilean earthquake of 1960, which measured 9.5 on the Richter scale, an area of 130 000 square kilometres was hit by 225 aftershock tremors. Many people preferred to live outdoors, for fear of collapsing buildings.

Twenty-eight aftershocks, 10 of them powerful, followed the 1964 Alaskan earthquake.

GO FACT!

DID YOU KNOW?

The 1997 earthquake in Assisi, Italy was relatively minor, but about 20 aftershocks caused lots of damage. The quake measured 5.6 on the Richter scale. The famous St. Francis of Assisi Basilica was badly damaged when its ceiling collapsed, killing four people.

Landslides, Fires, Floods and Tsunamis

Landslides, fires, floods and tsunamis often cause more death and destruction than the original earthquake.

Landslides and avalanches

Earthquakes can lead to massive **avalanches** and landslides. Tonnes of soil, rock and snow that are dislodged hurl down mountains and can bury villages, towns and cities.

Fires

Earthquakes cause fires when gas mains burst and electrical wires topple. Major earthquakes can also break water pipes and disrupt water supplies. This makes fighting fires difficult, if not impossible.

Floods

Landslides that block and thus change the course of rivers, can cause earthquake-related floods. Some earthquakes have also caused dam walls to crack and collapse, leading to massive flooding.

Tsunamis

Tsunamis are giant waves caused by underwater earthquakes or volcanoes. Travelling at up to 800 km per hour (500 miles per hour), tsunamis in the open sea may be less than half a metre high and barely noticeable. But as they reach shore, the shallow sea floor slows them down and forces them up to great heights.

Most of the 123 000 victims of Japan's Great Kanto earthquake of 1923 were killed by fires that swept through the city.

In 1970 an avalanche triggered by an earthquake, measuring 7.9 on the Richter scale, buried the town of Yungay, Peru. It killed all but 92 of the 20 000 inhabitants.

An earthquake in India in 1950, measuring 8.6 on the Richter scale, destroyed a dam on the Brahmaputra River, leading to the flooding of over 110 000 square kilometres (42 471 square miles).

GO FACT!

DID YOU KNOW?

The word 'tsunami' comes from the Japanese language and means 'giant harbour wave'.

Indian Ocean Tsunami

A tsunami is a large wave caused by an undersea earthquake. On December 26th 2004, an earthquake measuring 9.0 on the Richter scale occurred under the Indian Ocean, off the coast of Indonesia. The earthquake unleashed the deadliest tsunami in modern history, killing over 200 000 people in 14 countries.

How it all began

The build-up of giant forces, deep within the Earth, took hundreds of years. They were suddenly released on Boxing Day 2004. The earthquake occurred along an undersea fault line off the coast of the Indonesian island of Sumatra. The violent movement of two tectonic plates resulted in the sea floor rising 10 metres. This upward movement **displaced** billions of tonnes of water, creating a massive tsunami which travelled across the Indian Ocean at 800 kilometres per hour (500 miles per hour), the speed of a commercial airliner.

When the tsunami hit

Fifteen minutes after the earthquake, the first wave – nearly 20 metres high – crashed into the Indonesian island of Sumatra, demolishing everything in its path. The city of Banda Aceh was almost totally destroyed, killing countless thousands within minutes. The tsunami then continued on to Thailand. A 10 metre high wave killed thousands and caused billions of pounds of damage. Waves also headed west toward Sri Lanka and India. Without warning, the waves surged inland, like giant tides. Fourteen countries were affected by the Indian Ocean Tsunami.

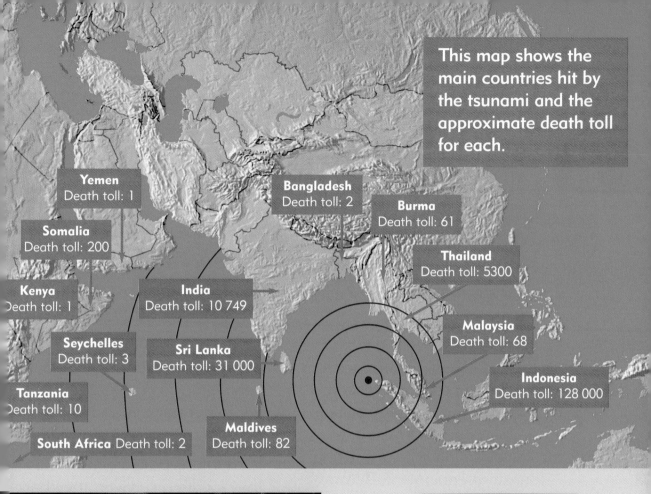

This map shows the main countries hit by the tsunami and the approximate death toll for each.

Yemen Death toll: 1

Bangladesh Death toll: 2

Burma Death toll: 61

Somalia Death toll: 200

Thailand Death toll: 5300

Kenya Death toll: 1

India Death toll: 10 749

Malaysia Death toll: 68

Seychelles Death toll: 3

Sri Lanka Death toll: 31 000

Indonesia Death toll: 128 000

Tanzania Death toll: 10

South Africa Death toll: 2

Maldives Death toll: 82

One of the classic warning signs of an approaching tsunami is the sea disappearing off the beaches. This occurred in Thailand, and people were curiously looking at the exposed seabed. When the waves hit, over 5 000 people were killed.

GO FACT!

DID YOU KNOW?

The Indian Ocean earthquake was the second biggest earthquake in recorded history. It generated the most devastating tsunami in modern times.

Rescue!

Though earthquakes can kill thousands of people, many survive. Some survivors are trapped under rubble, often with severe injuries. This leads to urgent rescue efforts.

Rescue efforts can range from the **frantic** efforts of dazed survivors pulling away bricks, timber and other rubble, to well-coordinated plans, using sensitive equipment. Before the emergency services arrive, survivors are often found by searchers who hear their cries for help. Once emergency plans are in action, teams of rescuers **methodically** search for survivors.

Electronic people detectors and specially trained dogs are two of the more **sophisticated** methods of finding survivors. Rescuers use detectors to listen for the sounds of people trapped in collapsed buildings. The detectors can pick up human heartbeats, and distinguish between the sounds made by people moving under the rubble and other background noises.

Sniffer dogs are trained to smell for humans buried alive. When they locate a survivor, they bark to alert the rescuers.

People rarely survive more than three days if trapped without food or water following an earthquake, so speedy rescue efforts are very important. Often the army is called in to help emergency workers.

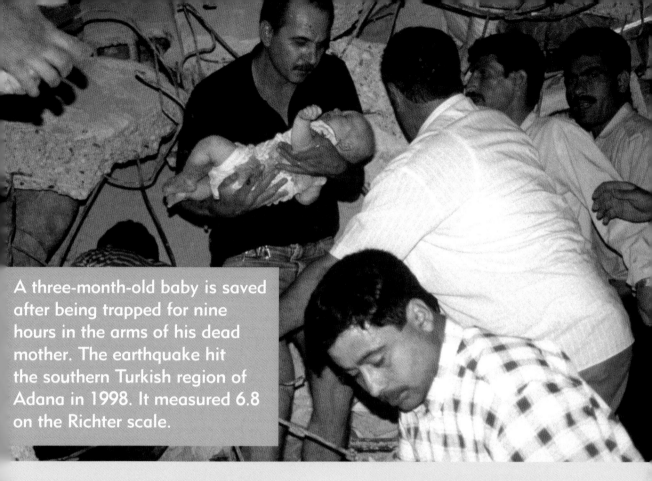

A three-month-old baby is saved after being trapped for nine hours in the arms of his dead mother. The earthquake hit the southern Turkish region of Adana in 1998. It measured 6.8 on the Richter scale.

Members of the Indonesian armed forces were brought into the Banda Ache earthquake zone to help rescue survivors.

Case Study – Kobe, Japan

Three tectonic plates lie underneath the islands of Japan. The movement of these plates makes Japan one of the most earthquake-prone places on Earth.

1995 earthquake

Early in the morning of 17th January 1995, the historic Japanese city of Kobe was hit by a powerful earthquake measuring 6.9 on the Richter scale. Buildings collapsed and fires quickly spread from **ruptured** gas pipes. Terrified citizens hid under whatever shelter they could find,

or rushed out into the shuddering streets. Many of the traditional wooden houses in Kobe's centre fell to pieces or ignited, while modern apartment buildings near the harbour collapsed.

When the 20 seconds of shaking ceased, over 170 000 buildings were destroyed. Fires burned out of control for the next 24 hours. Efforts to control the blazes were hampered by damage to the water supply.

By the time the worst of the disaster was over, more than 43 000 people had been injured and 6435 killed. 140 fires destroyed 100 hectares of the city, and over 300 000 people were left homeless. Rebuilding Kobe took 10 years and cost around $150 billion (£79 billion)

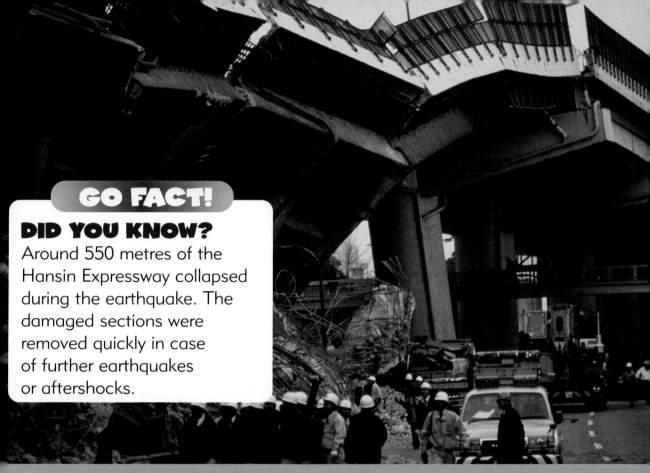

DID YOU KNOW?
Around 550 metres of the
Hansin Expressway collapsed
during the earthquake. The
damaged sections were
removed quickly in case
of further earthquakes
or aftershocks.

Parts of Kobe's rail system
collapsed during the earthquake.

Some survivors of the earthquake
spent five days trapped in cold,
frightening conditions before
being rescued.

19

Living with Earthquakes

As the world's population increases, more and more people live with the threat of earthquakes. There is nothing we can do to prevent earthquakes, but we can prepare for them.

Earthquake drills

In earthquake-prone areas such as Japan and California, schoolchildren regularly perform earthquake drills. They learn to follow techniques such as **duck and cover**, and the importance of not panicking if caught in an earthquake.

Japan

In especially earthquake-prone parts of Japan, children also carry safety helmets and oxygen masks. This will protect them from two of the most dangerous elements of earthquakes – falling debris and smoke from fires.

Disaster emergency plans

Governments in earthquake areas prepare disaster emergency plans. These plans assess the danger of earthquake-related disasters such as fires, floods and landslides. Authorities also attempt to limit the damage by maintaining strict building codes.

In some countries such as Turkey and Iran, which are also earthquake-prone, very little money is spent on prevention and planning. As a result, the death toll from earthquakes in these regions tends to be much higher. Over 26 000 people died in an earthquake on December 26th 2003 in Bam, Iran.

On September 1st, the anniversary of the Great Kanto earthquake of 1923, all 12 million residents of Tokyo take part in a city-wide earthquake drill.

GO FACT!

DID YOU KNOW?

Buildings on solid bedrock or tightly-packed soil have a better chance of surviving an earthquake than those built on loose soil or reclaimed land.

If caught in an earthquake, there are things you can do to protect yourself. If inside, move away from windows and doors, and shelter under a solid piece of furniture, such as a table. If outside, go to an open space, keeping away from buildings, trees and power lines.

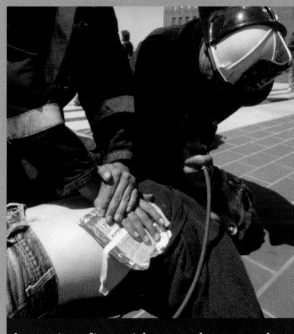

Learning first-aid procedures such as mouth-to-mouth resuscitation can help people to survive an earthquake.

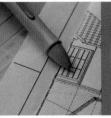

Building for Earthquake Saftey

Falling debris and collapsing buildings cause damage, injury and death. Building standards in many earthquake zones are very strict.

The importance of building for earthquake safety is clearly shown by two similar-sized earthquakes that occurred in 1988 and 1989. The American city of San Francisco has very strict building codes. Sixty-two people died when an earthquake, measuring 6.9 on the Richter scale, hit in 1989. The nation of Armenia in south western Asia does not have such strict codes, and when an earthquake measuring 6.8 hit in 1988, over 100 000 people lost their lives.

After an earthquake, engineers study which structures suffered the least damage and why. Architects can then use these reports to design new buildings.

The building industry in wealthier countries is constantly researching and improving building codes. In the Kobe earthquake of 1995 most buildings constructed after 1980 withstood the violent shaking of the earthquake.

Structural features that help withstand the violent shaking of an earthquake include:

1. deep, solid foundations

2. strong, but flexible steel frames

3. a low centre of gravity

4. **flexible** upper floors that allow the building to sway with the tremors.

It is more expensive to build earthquake-resistant structures, so poorer nations are hit hardest when an earthquake strikes.

The Transamerica Pyramid building in San Francisco shook for over a minute during the 1989 earthquake, but was not damaged.

The pyramid-shaped pagodas of Asia are fairly resistant to earthquakes because of their low centre of gravity.

GO FACT!
DID YOU KNOW?
San Francisco has some of the strictest building codes in the world.

23

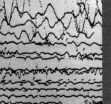

Earthquakes occur where tectonic plates interact, so monitoring these areas can tell us when stress is building up in the rock. This can indicate that an earthquake is likely to happen but it cannot tell us exactly when.

Seismometers and seismographs

Although it is impossible to predict when an earthquake will happen there are instruments such as seismometers that measure vibrations in the ground. As they record the tiniest of movements, seismometers can detect the minor vibrations that often occur just before a big quake. Often there is not enough time to evacuate areas before the earthquake strikes, but authorities can be warned to prepare. The **digital** information recorded by seismometers is turned into a **visual** record on a seismograph.

seismograph

Seismographs display the vibrations caused by an earthquake as a series of lines.

The Richter scale

The total energy released by an earthquake is measured on the Richter scale. The scale is used to compare the magnitude of earthquakes ranging from 1.0 to 10. An earthquake that measures 6.0 on the Richter scale makes 10 times more ground movement than one that measures 5.0. But more importantly, the level 6.0 earthquake releases much more energy – 32 times more than the level 5.0. The amount of energy released increases the destructive power of the earthquake.

Because of the recorded build-up of stress, scientists predict that Tokyo, San Francisco and Los Angeles are all due for major earthquakes in the future – possibly within the next generation.

Frequency of Occurrence of Earthquakes

Descriptor	Magnitude	Average Annually
Great	8 and higher	1
Major	7 - 7.9	17
Strong	6 - 6.9	134
Moderate	5 - 5.9	1319
Light	4 - 4.9	13 000
Minor	3 - 3.9	130 000
Very minor	2 - 2.9	1 300 000

The Richter scale is named after Charles Richter, who invented the scale in the 1930s.

A scientist who studies earthquakes is called a seismologist.

Make a Seismograph

You can make your own seismograph to record P, S and surface waves. Just follow the steps below to create and record your own earthquake.

What you need:

- large jar with a lid
- roll of paper
- pen
- sticky tape
- desk or table

What to do:

1 Place the roll of paper on the table or desk.

2 Fill the jar with water. Tape the pen to the jar, and put it on the paper roll so the tip of the pen touches the paper.

3 Pull the paper out slowly so the pen draws a straight line.

4 As one person continues to pull the paper out, the other gently shakes the table from side to side. This will form a line representing P-waves.

5 Shake the table harder – these larger lines represent S-waves.

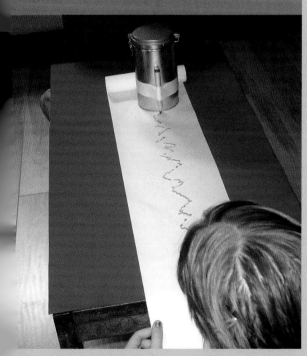

6 Shake the table harder again – these long and jagged lines represent surface waves.

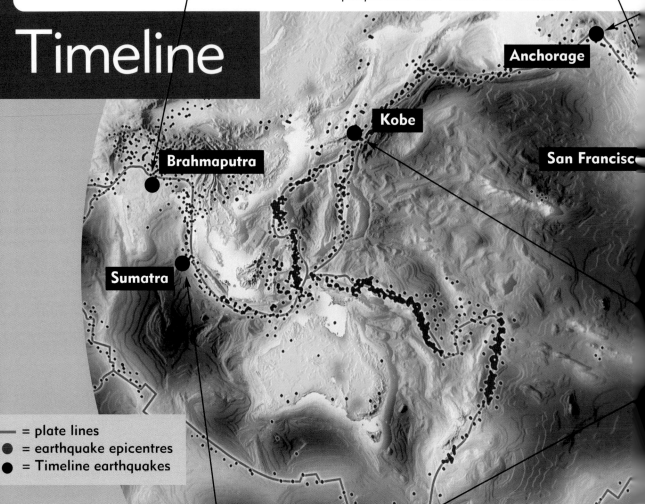

1950 Brahmaputra, India
An earthquake measuring 8.6 caused a dyke on the Brahmaputra river to burst. Waves 7 metres high submerged several villages and killed over 500 people.

1960 Chile
This earthquake, which measured 9.5 on the Richter scale, is the largest earthquake ever recorded. Tsunamis generated by the earthquake hit the coasts of such faraway places as New Guinea, New Zealand, the Philippines and Japan. Despite the strength of the earthquake more people died as a result of the tsunamis.

Timeline

Anchorage

Kobe

Brahmaputra

San Francisco

Sumatra

— = plate lines
● = earthquake epicentres
● = Timeline earthquakes

2004 Sumatra, Indian Ocean
Measuring 9.0 on Richter scale, this quake caused the most destructive tsunami in modern times. It is estimated that over 200 000 people died as a result of the earthquake and tsunami combined.

1998 Adana, Turkey
Apartment blocks collapsed when this quake jolted the region. Over 100 people died, and thousands were injured. The quake was followed by 16 aftershocks, causing widespread damage to buildings. It measured 6.3 on the Richter scale.

1964 Anchorage, Alaska, USA
Measuring 9.2 on the Richter scale, this is the largest ever recorded earthquake in the USA. It resulted in 131 deaths.

1970 Yungay, Peru
This earthquake, measuring 7.9 on the Richter scale, was the worst natural disaster in Peru's history. It caused huge landslides and killed over 40 000 people.

1988 Armenia
Due to poor building standards, hospitals and schools collapsed. The freezing winter temperatures hampered rescue efforts. Over 25 000 lost their lives. The earthqake measured 6.8 on the Richter scale.

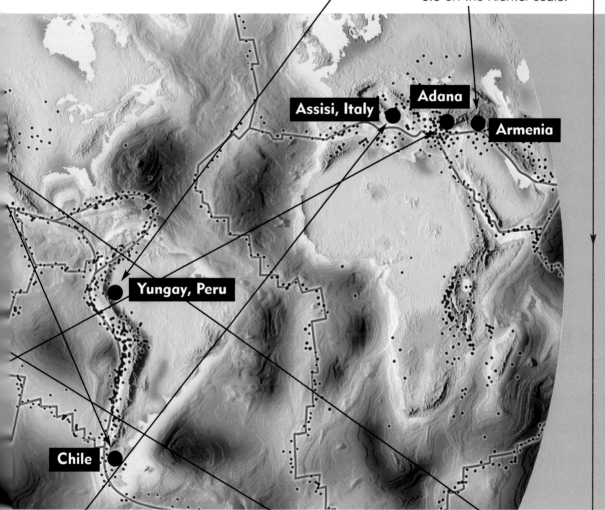

Assisi, Italy

Adana

Armenia

Yungay, Peru

Chile

97 Assisi, Italy
ver 100 people were injured d 11 died as a result of ling buildings. Priceless art asures were also destroyed the earthquake and its ershocks. It measured 5.6 the Richter scale.

1995 Kobe, Japan
This was the second worst earthquake in Japan's history. The Great Kanto earthquake of 1923 was the worst Japan experienced. In the Kobe earthquake over 6000 people died. It measured 6.9 on the Richter scale.

1989 San Francisco
A major earthquake measuring 7.1 on the Richter scale, it caused major damage to roads and took the lives of over 60 people. Most people died when a major freeway collapsed.

Earthquakes

When	Where	What happened?
2200 BC	Sodom and Gomorrah	Both cities sank below the Dead Sea.
365	Alexandria, Egypt	Alexandria's lighthouse, one of the Seven Wonders of the Ancient World, was destroyed. Earthquake killed 5000 people.
1169	Sicily, Italy	Mount Etna erupted, causing an earthquake. Both disasters claimed 15 000 lives.
1556	Shannxi Province, China	The most destructive earthquake ever recorded. Claimed over 800 000 victims.
1611	Honshu, Japan	Three thousand people died. The tsunami that followed the earthquake flooded the area and created a new, permanent lake.
1755	Lisbon, Portugal	Earthquake, tsunami and fire caused near total destruction of Lisbon. Over 70 000 people died.
1906	San Francisco, USA	The fires following this earthquake burned out of control for three days and destroyed two-thirds of the city.
1923	Honshu, Japan	An earthquake destroyed over 600 000 homes, with the fires that followed killing most of the 143 000 victims.
1931	New Zealand	New Zealand's largest recorded earthquake killed 256 people and lifted the land surrounding the town of Napier by 2 metres.
1972	Nicaragua	Worst earthquake in country's history killed 7000 people and left 200 000 homeless.
1976	Tangshan, China	One of the worst earthquakes in modern times in terms of loss of life. Official Chinese figures estimate 250 000 people died, though other sources think over three times that number died.
1985	Mexico City, Mexico	An earthquake lasting for three minutes left a million people homeless and 10 000 dead in Mexico's capital city. A strong aftershock the following day added to the damage and death tol
1989	Newcastle, Australia	One of the few major earthquakes to hit Australia, this caused the deaths of 13 people and extensive damage to the city's centre.
1999	Chi-Chi, Taiwan	Nearly 2500 people lost their lives. Extensive damage done to bridges and roads.

Glossary

avalanches large amounts of ice and snow that break away and fall or slide down the side of a mountain

brittle easily broken or snapped

digital information recorded or represented in number form

displaced put out of usual place; removed from proper place

duck and cover a method of protection where you duck down, curl yourself up and cover your head

epicentre the point on the Earth's surface that is directly above the point where an earthquake originates

estimated a rough calculation

fault lines cracks in the Earth's crust, where pressure is created as the sides of tectonic plates rub against each other

flexible something that is easily bent

focus the point on a fault line where rock breaks causing an earthquake

frantic wild with fear, pain, excitement

immense very large

intensity a measure of the strength of an earthquake

magma extremely hot molten rock occurring beneath the Earth's crust

magnitude a measure of the size of an earthquake

methodically to do something in an orderly, organised way

monitor check, observe or record something

ruptured broken or burst

seismograph an instrument which measures vibrations within the Earth's surface

sophisticated showing a high degree of skill

stress a load or force that produces a strain

subterranean located or existing beneath the Earth's surface

tectonic plates moving pieces of

tsunami large waves caused by an undersea earthquake

visual something which can be seen

31

Index